ALEXA
MANAGEMENT
FOR **NEWCOMERS**

Alexa for beginners: using Alexa with
Echo Dot, Show, Spot, Connect, and
Amazon Tap

Stephen W. Rock

Dedicated to all my readers

Acknowledgement

Ii want to say a very big thank you to Michael Lime, a 3D builder, my colleague. He gave me moral support throughout the process of writing this book.

Table of Contents

Introduction 9

Chapter 1..10

What is Alexa? 10

What can I use Alexa with? 11

What can Alexa do for you?................................12

Chapter 2 14

Alexa tips and tricks..14

Create a profile for everyone 15

Change Alexa wake word...................................16

Clear your voice data 17

Include other devices...18

Stream that music with the Bluetooth 19

Simultaneously stream audio across all your Echos ..20

Using your voice to add some skills 21

Using the voice remote 22

The intercom feature for broadcast 23

Ordering from Amazon Prime............................24

Use Alexa to make calls and messages.............25

Get notification for delivery 26

Receive special Prime deals...............................28

Use a different music player.................................29

Changing the accent...................................30

Tell Alexa to repeat what she said...........................31

Make Alexa wake you up with a more thrilling song.32

Use Alexa to listen to Podcasts...................................33

Setting your own voice profiles...........................34

Turn Alexa to a mathematician..............................35

Make Routines...............................36

Enable the wake up sound...........................37

Get a night light with the Echos ring.........................38

Using your computer to get access to Alexa...........39

Using Alexa from the amazon app...........................40

Get rid of an Alexa device.................................41

Creating reminders with Alexa...........................42

Using Alexa for coffee..............................43

Say several commands together..........................44

Cancel Alexa's 'Okay'.............................45

Resetting the Echo..................................46

Chapter 3.................................47

Setting Up and Personalizing Your Alexa Device.......47

How to change Alexa voice............................51

Chapter 4...................................53

Using Alexa to Play Music on Your Home Bluetooth Speakers 53

Chapter 5 56

Using Alexa to watch videos 56

Chapter 6 58

How to Unlock Alexa Skills 58

Chapter 7 60

How to Turn Your Home to a Smart Home with Alexa
.... 60

Chapter 8 63

Using Alexa on your Amazon Echo Dot 63

Chapter 9 66

Using Alexa on Echo Show 66

Chapter 10.. 69

Using Alexa on your Amazon Tap 69

Chapter 11 72

Using Alexa on Echo Connect 72

Chapter 12 75

Using Echo Spot with Alexa 75

Chapter 13..78

Fun Things to do with Alexa 78

Chapter 14..85

Alexa Troubleshooting 85

Alexa doesn't connect to devices 86

Alexa doesn't respond to calling.................................. 88

Alexa doesn't stream.. 89

Alexa cut offs form Wi-Fi connection 90

Alexa isn't hearing you well... 91

Alarm sounds that Alexa gives are too loud............... 92

Alexa doesn't connect Bluetooth 93

Trouble with Spotify 94

Alexa activates by itself.. 95

Disclaimer... 96

About the author 97

Introduction

The title of this book already gives a hint on what the book is about. It is a guide for those who are eager to explore the wonders of Alexa, Amazon's voice assistant.

Readers will be introduced into Alexa proper, learn Alexa setup and operation, and be taught through basic troubleshooting.

Also, readers will learn how to configure and customize Alexa to work with Echo Spot, Echo Show, Echo Dot, Echo Connect, Amazon Tap, etc.

Eventually, you'll come to when you'll see several Alexa commands for TV, music and Easter eggs.

The content of this book are well presented. Steps are outlined to make it easier for readers to identify what to do and how to go about it without any distraction.

This is just another superb user guide from the author's stable. Read and explore

Chapter 1
What is Alexa?

Alexa is a voice assistant from Amazon. To put simply, Alexa is that voice you hear from Amazon speakers like Echo or Echo Dot. Just as how you use Siri with apple products, so you use Alexa with Amazon Echos.

With Alexa, you get to ask questions like 'what's the weather like today'. Alexa was made to sound like a real person. Like as if you're having a conversation with somebody. In fact you could even get her to tell a joke. To get her to perform tasks, you just have to have to say the right commands. Saying the word **Alexa** will trigger the voice assistant then you can give out commands

You can use Alexa as long as you've got an Echo, Echo spot, Echo Dot. In fact you could even use Alexa with an Amazon Fire TV. If you like calling her Alexa, you can just leave it at that, but Amazon gives users the opportunity to change the wake word for the assistant. You could either change it to Echo or you could choose Amazon.

What can I use Alexa with?

As said earlier, you can use Alexa with Amazon Echo devices like the Echo Show and the Echo Dot. But it's not only with Amazon devices; you can also use Alexa to control some third-party.

Like the InstaView refrigerator, or your lights, your thermostat, your door looks, you fans, coffee maker and so many devices. With Alexa you like is made easier by just saying the word. Imagine how easy it is for you to just lay in your bed and say 'Alexa, lock the garage door'

It's not hard to control these things as long as you use smart home systems. Like Smart things, Wink or the Logitech harmony.

What can Alexa do for you?

With Alexa, she can you can get daily news and the scores of your favourite sport, offer information, play you music when you give the command. You can also use it to find out the weather situation and do cool stuffs with your smart home devices.

But you should know that Alexa a capable of more and not only telling you weather forecasts and giving answers to general questions. She can help you do stuff that will make you feel like you're living in 2050 already.

For example you can use it to do routines. Well, routines in the Alexa language means that she performs some tasks when you say just one command. Le for example you can get her to tell you the weather and your schedule by just say something along the lines of 'Alexa, good morning'

You can also use Alexa to help you out in translation. Like if you have this word and you would like to know what it sounds like in another language, you can just use Alexa. She can translate to over 30 languages by using the Translates skill. Once you have enabled the skill, you can get her to translate a word for you by saying 'Alexa, open Translated' then 'how do you say MY NAME IS in Spanish?'

You can also use it to announce something through other Echo devices. You can also use Alexa to shop. You can add items to your cart or buy them from the Amazon website.

Chapter 2
Alexa tips and tricks

NOTES:

Create a profile for everyone

For those who have a lot of people in the house using Amazon accounts, you can just include them in your own Alexa household profile. If you want to know the profile that it is switched to already, you could ask Alexa. You say 'Alexa, which profile is this?'

If it is in someone else profile and you would like to change it to you own, you just say the word. You don't fiddle with anything thing in the settings you just say 'Alexa, switch profiles'.

You should know though that if you have another member, something like your shopping to do lists isn't kept separately. But they still have the access to use your Prime account to be able to shop and order stuff. The good thing is that you can share content libraries.

Change Alexa wake word

Can you imagine how awkward it would sound if someone bears the name **Alexa** in your home. Or let's even leave out the humans, what if it was your pet and you say 'Alexa get off the couch now'. So you don't get Amazon Alexa wondering what in the world you're talking about, it's best you change the name.

But what's not nice about this is that you can't set the name you wish. Amazon gives you a list of names and you can only choose from those. The worst part is that are only 4 options Alexa, Echo, Amazon and Computer. If those names sound nice to you and you want to select it,

1. Enter the **Alexa app**
2. Go to **Settings**
3. Select your Echo
4. Tap **wake word**
5. Select the name you which
6. Hit **Save**

Clear your voice data

Okay here's a secret you've never heard of before. You know how you browse on Google and they store the information you searched with them. Yeah the same creepy thing happens with Alexa. All what you say and request to Alexa is sent to the servers and of course stored.

And I'm pretty sure that the idea of your voice recording being stored in the clouds sounds creepy to your so the best course of action is to delete em all. TO do so,

1. Grip a computer, enter a browser and search **amazon.com/myx**
2. You'll have to sign
3. Select **Your Devices**
4. Look for your Echo device from the option it presents
5. Tap menu **3- dot** icon next to it
6. Hit **Manage voice recording**
7. Choose **Delete.**

Include other devices

With Alexa you can control you smart home devices with just your mouth. But before you can live in the future like this, you have to make sure that your smart home device supports Alexa. But not all smart-home support Alexa

But that doesn't mean you cannot use Alexa. You have to first find out if there's a Alexa skill for hat smart-home device. If you don't see it, you'll have to check some other sites like **IFTTT** with **Yonomi**. From those sites, you'll be able to check if you smart home devices is supported. With these two services, you need to know how to make use of them well as they can make Alexa more efficient.

Stream that music with the Bluetooth

When you arm yourself with some Echo Or Echo Dot, you have the power to automatically listen to audio books from Audible, Pandora, Amazon Prime and Spotify. Even radio services like TuneIn Radio and iHeartRadio. If you're not satisfied with the audiobooks from audible, you can just get Alexa to read to you. She can read Kindle books to you, you just have to say the word.

But for the fans of Google Play music or Apple music, you're not left out. You can just use Bluetooth to pair your smartphone or computer with your Echo and steam. This also works for other audio libraries that are not supported.

Simultaneously stream audio across all your Echos

Recently, we got the announcement from Amazon that an update was coming out. It's the update that allows users to play music to different speakers. Yep if you've got many Echos in your home, you can sync them all and blow the roof.

You just have to use the feature that's like Sonos and make an Audio Group. You do this from the Alexa app. Once you've created the group you just tell Alexa to play a song with that group.

Using your voice to add some skills

Previously, if you want to add silks to your Echos, you'll have to dig in the Alexa app, or go through the Echo Amazon site. When you enter, you now search or te skill and them add them manually. This process might seem normal because that what were used too. But were living in the future now, aren't we. We use our voices.

Adding skills with your voices is really not hard. If you know the skill name, 'Alexa, enable (skill name)' You just wait a couple of seconds you'll be able to use the just enabled skill. This process is really easy and makes the job fast..

Using the voice remote

It's not every time you'll have the Echo near you, sometimes you might be in the kitchen and the Echo is sitting around in the living room. You don't always have to go near it before you can actually give it command. Why not check out the Amazon Echo Voice Remote. Should be around 30$.

This remote works fine with the Echo dot and Echo but not for the Tap. You just go to the **settings** in the Alexa app and pair the remote to your Echo. This will enable you to access Alexa from other rooms. In fact you could use the remote from outside. You should note though, that the range of this remote is kind of limited, so you don't want to travel to mars

The intercom feature for broadcast

This one too is really useful if you've got a lot of Echo speakers in the house. Like if there's one in the living room and one in the bedroom, you can use the feature for intercom to communicate with the speakers. Let say you just made dinner and you want the house to know food is ready, just use the Echo as an intercom.

You could start with 'Alexa, drop in the bedroom' then you'll say what you want to announce and it will be broadcasted across the speakers

Ordering from Amazon Prime

You have the opportunity of ordering about millions of items, all you have to do is ask. Before, users were only able to re-order products you've purchased with Prime.

But now, if an item is eligible for prime, you can order it. In fact, you'll be able to ask for a ride from Uber or even order a Dominos Pizza

Use Alexa to make calls and messages

Recently, Echos got the upgrade of sending messages and making calls. But this is only with Alexa users. Fi there's someone that is on your lists of contact and he has an Echo device (Echo Show, Echo Dot, Echo) you can call and message tem if they have enabled calling.

You just have to say the word. 'Alexa, call Miley' or 'Alexa send Emma a message. The all will ring in their Echo devices with the Alexa app.

Get notification for delivery

Among the many improvements Alexa has gotten is the ability to get notifications for both the calls and messages you missed. Users were able to receive notifications about updates and other skills.

Users are also able to get notifications about their deliveries for their orders with Amazon Prime. If what you order is ready to be delivered, your Echo will notify you and show a yellow light.

To make this notification show, you'll have to go to the Alexa app.
1. Open up the Alexa app
2. Move to the **settings**
3. Then select **Accounts**
4. Choose **Notifications**
5. Then **Shopping Notifications**. Turn it on.

With this, skills will be able to send notifications. If you want to find out the notifications that you've received, you can just ask Alexa, 'Alexa, what are my notifications. Or rather than the plain old language, you could spice it up and say 'Alexa, what did I miss?'

Receive special Prime deals

You know how much you spent on your Echo or Echos if you have plenty. Among their competitors you chose to patronize them. Amazon recognizes this fact and they like to show some love to the dedicated customers who have decided to use their hard earned money to buy their products.

Every now and then, Amazon prepares exclusive deals specially kept for only those who have purchased speakers that use Alexa. There was this deal that made the Amazon Echo Dot and the Tap available to only those who have purchased an Echo.

That was in the past, in recent times Amazon gave a Prime Day deal for only Alexa users. So these deals were only for those who owned Official Alexa devices. This deal did not include third party Alexa devices.

Use a different music player

Alexa and Echos are made by Amazon. So it's only normal that the music player set as default is the Amazon Music. But that does not mean that the only music player you can use is the default one. For those who have favourite music service, you can just switch to that.

TO switch to your other much players,
1. Enter the **Alexa app**
2. Select **Settings**
3. In Alexa preferences, choose **Music & Media**
4. Select **Choose Default Music Services**

You'll be able to switch it to a number of music services like Spotify, iHeartRadio, Pandora or TuneIn Radio.

Changing the accent

It is true that Alexa can understand voices well. You just have to enunciate your words and she'll be able to hear you requests. But it's not all humans say that she can understand, at least if you not set it like that first. You may speak the same language she understands but with a different accent.

The best thing to do Is to change Alexa's accent.
1. Fire up the Alexa app
2. Tap Settings
3. Select the device
4. Choose Language
5. Select from the options it presents

Tell Alexa to repeat what she said

You know those times when you ask for something and your mind is not even paying attention to the answer you're given? Yea, it can happen with Alexa to. It true that she says her words slowly and meticulously, but sometimes you may not be paying attention to what she tells you.

Of course you could just say your request again but you don't have to say such lengthy words all over again. You could just conveniently say 'Alexa can you say that again' or you could still say Alexa, can you repeat that' And that will get her telling you her most recent reply. She would answer you without any brilliant remarks

Make Alexa wake you up with a more thrilling song

You know those lame alarm wake calls. Some do not even wake deep sleepers. But one nice tip you can try with Alexa is let her do the work. Yu can make her use a particular track, or an album or playlist to wake you up. In fact you could set her to wake you up with a radio station.

Like the other tricks, you just have to say the word. This time it's 'Alexa, wake me up to (say the song title r radio satin name) at 5:00 am.

Use Alexa to listen to Podcasts

For those who are drawn to podcasts, Alexa an also do you well in that aspect. And yes you could use Alexa podcast ability but you could still pay no attention to that and use something else instead with your Echo like the skill called AnyPod

With this you're able to listen to podcasts easily. The episodes of the podcasts will play in an orderly way. And in fact if you stop listening to it and you want to open it up again, it will start from where you stopped last time. Say 'Alexa, enable AnyPod skill'

Setting your own voice profiles

Okay, earlier we discussed how you connect different profiles to an echo. But that all you can do regarding profiles. You also create voice profiles. Okay, you didn't quite understand that. What voice profiles means is that Alexa will be able to tell different voices apart. She can identify who is speaking and whose profiles it belongs to.

So if Johnny asks 'Alexa, what's on my calendar' Alexa will tell Johnny the events on his own calendar. And if Lily says to play music, she will play the music according to Lily's taste.

Turn Alexa to a mathematician

Using Alexa to control your smart home is very easy and sweet to. All you need is your voice. You don't have to dig in apps and try to turn of light or control fans. And while that is convenient, there's something else you can make Alexa do for you.

You can tell Alexa to do calculations. You can tell her to convert different currencies. She is also able to convert measurements. In terms of mathematical equations you could say 'Alexa, 23 x 58'. To covert you could say 'Alexa, 45 pound to dollars'

Make Routines

When we say Routines we mean a feature that makes Alexa be able to complete several actions with one command. One nice example to explain this routine more is when you're about o sleep.

You could say 'Alexa, Good night' and the front door will be locked, the lights will be turned off and your thermostat will be adjusted to a suitable temperature. Talk about living in the future.

1. GO to Alexa app
2. Tap routines
3. Follow the instructions it gives.

You can edit it but customization settings are limited. There are not too many actions you can do for now. We hope that in future it will be expanded.

Enable the wake up sound

There's this cool feature that enables you to issue commands to Alexa rather quickly. With this you need not wait for the Alexa light to turn on before you can say your command or as your question. You don't have to pause when saying 'Alexa, lock the garage doors'

If you're not close to your Echo it will be best for you to set an audio notifications to notify you if Alexa was listen to you

1. Slide in the **Alexa App**
2. Choose **Settings**
3. Select the name of your Echo
4. Tap **Sounds**
5. Turn on the option for **Wake-Up sound**
6. Switch on **End of request sound**

Get a night light with the Echos ring

On your Alexa speaker, you have a light ring. This can tell you many information and notifications like if you missed a call or the level of the volume. But there's a skill that can enable you to use the light as a ring light.

After you've enabled the skill, you can just say to Alexa 'Alexa, enable night light for 30 minutes'. This will turn on the light ring for as long as you say. And if you want to turn if of abruptly, you can say 'Alexa, stop'

Using your computer to get access to Alexa

One wonderful about Alexa is that you don't really need to have an Echo speaker before you can use her capabilities. You could just do it with a web browser. That's no hassle to get.

1. Open up your web browser
2. Search Echosim.io and sign in to your Amazon account
3. If you want to access Alexa, just click the microphone button and ask your question or say command

You can get many off the features of Alexa from here. Like you can have control of your smart devices and enable some skills. But you should know that you cannot stream audio.

Using Alexa from the amazon app

Previously, in the amazon app, you get the voice search function. But now it's been replaced. And yeah of course, it's now Alexa. With it you can ask for information and do conversion.

If you want to use this

1. Enter the Amazon app either on Android or iOS
2. Select the microphone next to the bar for search

You can ask interact with Alexa here just like you would on the hardware and yes you can stream music. You could even listen to podcast and audiobook

Get rid of an Alexa device

If you've tried to use one of these other ways to access Alexa or you've created your Alexa device, you'll find that you won't be able to remove them from your Amazon account through the Alexa app.

Well that doesn't mean you can do at all, it just that it's not available on the app. You have to go through the Amazon site.

1. Log in to your amazon account
2. Go to **Manage your content and devices**
3. Select your device and you'll be able to deregister it

Creating reminders with Alexa

With Alexa, you can now create reminders. Those times when you think that you would forget something you want to do like going to the market or checking what's boiling in the kitchen, you can just tell Alexa to remind you.

You could say something along the lines of 'Alexa, remind me to visit the grocery store tomorrow at 1 pm' When you do this, Alexa will give an alarm to remind you to get to the store. With Alexa, you don't have to say a specific word, you can diversify and say something like

'Alexa, reminders'
'Alexa what are my reminders this week'
'Alexa, remind me to call Jamie in two hours'

Using Alexa for coffee

Those regular visits to Starbucks should be reduced to an extent if you've got Alexa. You could just use Alexa to switch on the coffee maker and brew coffee with no stress. They are many coffee makers that can be controlled by Alexa.

For example **Behmor Connected brewer** is one wonderful machine that notices when the coffee gets low and reorders is with no delay. You could also check other cool machines that you could use via IFTTT.

Say several commands together

It's not easy to make Alexa do multiple tasks at once. She tends to turn off after you've called her name and said your command. To get her to do something else, you've got to call her with the wake word again and say the command. This is stressful in a way and takes time.

You can just turn on this cool new feature titled **Follow-up mode**. This mode is will allow you to say commands together. After you say the wake word, issue the command and wait for her to say **Okay** then say the next and repeat as many as you desire.

To signify that you're done with the commands, you could just say 'Stop' or you could be a bit more flexible and say like 'Thank you'. And then commands will be carried out

Cancel Alexa's 'Okay'

Something you should have noticed as you use your Echo is that if you issue out a command to Alexa, she tends to say 'Okay' if she's capable of carrying it out. But it's not everything you need to hear okay for you to know she heard your command. Like if you tell her to turn off the lights in the night, you don't need her to wake everyone up with her 'Okay'

To turn off this feature, you don't need to start digging in the settings you just say 'Alexa, turn of Brief mode' with this, her responses will be shorter and less noticeable. Like instead of shouting out 'Okay' she'll just signify with a sound

Resetting the Echo

Yeah you're living in the future but Alexa is technology and you know that no matter how dependable a tech can be it's sure to present some issues. Some issues are easy to solve, others will get you resetting the device.

But resetting is really no hassle. But first you just do something's as easy as unplugging the device and pugging it back in then connect to a network again. The problem should be gone now.

But if the problem is just too stubborn and still stays,
1. You could just grab a paper clip.
2. Look for the reset button that's at the bottom of the device and press it with it
3. You should see the light switch colors then go off. After a few seconds, it'll turn on again and the device should be reset.

Chapter 3
Setting Up and Personalizing Your Alexa Device

Now for those who just got their Echos, you know that there's no way you can start to use Alexa without actually setting it up. When you set it up, then you can use Alexa to play music, get weather reports, give you news, sports scores and a whole lot more.

The Echo is fully equipped with 7 mics. So you it can hear you anywhere you are in the room. But that does not mean you should go to mars and start yelling **Alexa**. If that's your plan then you might want to get a voice remote.

So let's get started with the step to set up you Alexa device.

Step 1

You first have to download the app. The Alexa app. You using Alexa so the only reasonable thing to do now is get her app. If you use an Apple tablet or phone, then you should make sure operates on iOS 9.0 or higher. For the android guys, should be Android 5.0 or higher. For fire, should be Fire OS 3 or higher.

Downloading it is no hassle. All you need is internet connection and you'll have to go to your devices app store and search for **Alexa app.** If you use a computer, then just connect to a network and go to the Amazon website for Alexa.

Step 2

If you thought that step was easy, then his one will probably be child's play. Your Echo does not need batteries to work. All it need to is to be connected to power regularly. So that mans that you just have to find a power outlet.

Connect the power adapter to your Alex device. And put the power adapter to a power outlet. For you to know that everything's fine, the ling ring on the Echo should show blue. After a few seconds, the light should become orange. This means that Alexa is ready to welcome you. After a few seconds you should hear Alexa tell you that the Echo is ready for set up.

Step 3

Now you'll have to connect your device to your Wi-Fi. If you use the latest Echo version, this process shouldn't break a sweat as you'll be told what to do to connect. But you know things may happen and the process can get stuck. All you have to do is enter the Alexa app on your smartphone or tablet.

From there search for all the networks that are available and select your Wi-Fi network. After you've connected to a network, you'll be asked if your Wi-Fi password should be saved to Amazon. If you want to connect another Echo device or connect it to smart home devices, this option will be really helpful.

There's also an option you might consider when your settings up your Wi-Fi, You'll be asked if you want to connect to a public network. But if you choose a public network, you want get the option on saving your password.

Step 4

Now here comes the fun part. Try talking to Alexa. You can start by just saying **Alexa**, that's the default name, you can also change it if there's another Alexa in your home and you don't want to cause commotion. To change it,

1. Enter the Alexa app
2. Select **help and feedback**
3. Choose change the wake word

That's the long route, you could just say 'Alexa, change the wake word'. I know you're hoping to be able to call her different names like 'T-bone' or 'Ciara'. But sadly, amazon only confines us to 'Computer', 'Echo and 'Amazon'

Enjoy your Echo

Yeah you're ready to start using Alexa. To test is everything is working fine and well, say 'Alexa, hello' If you're hear an 'Hello' from her, then everything's okay. But you didn't get your Echo just hear hello. You got it for fun things

If you go to the Alexa app, you see two features, called **Things to try** and **Skills & Games**. These are cool features you should try, like for example skills can help you to customize Alexa and allow her to do certain things that she can't normally do.

How to change Alexa voice

One cool personalization feature of Alexa is the ability to change her voice or accent. If speak British accent, you can make her speak like a Briton. In fact you could even change the language all together. You can change the languages to Japanese, Spanish, and German. This will be really cool you're from a place where the main language is not English.

1. Open up the Alexa app in your tablet or smartphone
2. Enter the **Settings**. It the icon with the gear symbol.
3. After the devices that are connected to Alexa shows up, tap the device you want to change the voice of
4. After selecting the device, Move downwards and tap **Language**.
5. The list of languages should show up. Select the language of your choice

After choosing your preferred language, you can have some fun testing out some other language or accents. After choosing the language, tap **Save changes**. Now if you give a command to Alexa, you'll hear her answer you in the language or accent you selected.

Chapter 4
Using Alexa to Play Music on Your Home Bluetooth Speakers

With your Alexa device, you can play music with your Favourite music player like Spotify or Pandora. But you should know that the sound that the Echo produces doesn't give you the best experience. Even with the newly created Echos, you still don't get a cool sound.

But then if you look beyond the Echo, and get yourself an awesome Bluetooth speaker, it's sure that you get a better audio quality. All it means is that you don't have to rely on the Echo's inbuilt speakers just connect it to an external speaker.

So before you can start to enjoy the external speaker, you'll have to make sure f a few things first.

- The speakers you're using should be a speaker that's Echo certified

- You want to make sure that the Bluetooth speakers and the Echo are not more than 3 feet away from each other.
- No other Bluetooth device should be connected to your Echo.

Now to connect and pair the duo

1. You want to set your Bluetooth speaker to pair. If you don't know how to do that, then you might have to visit the Bluetooth speakers manual or user guide.
2. Grab your smartphone or tablet and enter the Alexa app
3. Choose the icon for **Devices**
4. A list should show up now, it's the list containing the Echos connected to the Alexa app, choose the device you want to pair with the Bluetooth speaker
5. Choose the option for **Bluetooth Devices**
6. Then **Pair a new device**
7. Another list will pop up again. This contains the Bluetooth devices that the App can find. Choose you own Bluetooth speaker from the option and follow the directions it gives you.

Now if you've done this step to connect your Echo to the Bluetooth speaker, you don't have to start digging through the app, you can just easily say 'Alexa, connect'. Once you do that, Alexa will connect the Echo to the Bluetooth device that was recently connected to it. This only works if you've connected to the Bluetooth before.

Chapter 5
Using Alexa to watch videos

Now we're going to be using Alexa to watch videos. We're watching so we need screens. And you well know that an Echo doesn't have screen, neither does the Echo Dot. You'll need an Eco device that's enabled with screen to be able to watch videos with Alexa like the Echo Show

With Alexa, you can access the **Prime Video Library** and watch TV shows or movies. But it's not only amazon video service you can use, you can also try and connect to third-party video services. Tell your Echo device, 'Alexa, open videos'. You'll be able to choose a video provider from the option that shows up.

And for those who have connected their device to the Fire TV, Alexa can get confused (sort of) of where to play when you tell to play a video. She might play it on the Fire TV. So make sure to include the name of your Echo device at the end of every command.

You could say these to get Alexa to play a video
- 'Alexa, show me my video library
- 'Alexa, show me Michael Spanes movies
- 'Alexa, open videos
- 'Alexa show me my watch list
- 'Alexa, search for Hunter in the Snow'

Chapter 6
How to Unlock Alexa Skills

Alexa skills are abilities triggered by voice that sort of give Alexa superpowers. It is a cool way to personalize your Echo

If you want to get Alexa skills, you can search for It from the Alexa ap. Or you could go to the Amazon website and go the Alexa Skills Store. If there's a sill you know the name from memory, you can ask Alexa to enable it for you by saying 'Alexa, enable (name of skill)'

If you want to enable the skills from the Alexa app,

1. Enter the menu of the app
2. Tap **Skill & Games**
3. Look for a skill that you want to enable and tap it. Once you tap, you'll open up the detail's page for the skill. In the details page for the skill, you'll find different examples of the things you can say to Alexa to get to perform certain functions
4. Choose **Enable Skill**

Also you can also manage the skill you've enabled. You'll be able to personalize and tweak some of the settings. Like you can Manage permissions, accept whether the skill can send you notification and if you don't want to use the skill anymore, you can just select the Disable Skill option to disable it. You can also tell Alexa to do it for you by saying 'Alexa, disable (name of skill)

Chapter 7

How to Turn Your Home to a Smart Home with Alexa

Lights

You can find a lot of smart lights the market. A smart bulb like Lifx is one that makes set up easy and smooth.

1. Connect the bulb to the socket
2. Install the app for your lights (like the Lifx app).
3. Select the option to **Add bulbs** or a symbol for plus and you'll be able to connect the bulb to a Wi-Fi
4. In the Alexa app, select the skill for your lights
5. Choose **Smart home** in **menu**
6. Select **Devices**
7. Then **Discover,** the app should scan and look for the smart bulb

Thermostat

Thermostats like Nest can be great

1. Install the thermostat in your home
2. In the Alexa app, enter the **menu** and choose **skills**
3. Search and enable the skill for your Thermostats (like Nest Thermostat)
4. In the **menu**, Select **Smart home**
5. Choose **Devices** and select **Discover**
6. Once the app has discovered the thermostat, you can control it with Alexa

Fans

For fans, you can plug them to a smart plug and contort with the help of Alexa

1. Install the app of your smart plug (like the Kasa app)
2. Register account in the app and select the icon for smart plug
3. Connect the smart plug to a power outlet plug the fan to the smart plug. Go through with the instructions given in the app to link the plug with the app
4. Give a name to the smart pug, enable the option of **Remote control** and follow the

directions given to connect the smart plug to a wireless network.

5. Enter the Alexa app and search for the name of the skill
6. Choose **smart home**
7. Hit **Devices**, then choose **Discover**
8. After the app has discovered the smart plug, you'll be able give commands to it.

Other machines like electric water, coffee makers and other appliances can be plugged to a smart-plug and be controlled with Alexa.

Chapter 8
Using Alexa on your Amazon Echo Dot

Okay so you just got your new Echo Dot, it's time to start enjoying its awesome feature, but you should know that before you can start to do anything meaningful with the device, you've got to set up Alexa. Alexa is like the brains of the Echo Dot that you can tell to perform stuffs for you.

With your Echo Dot, you don't have screen, so you'll have to grab your phone or tablet to set it up. Look for the Amazon Alexa app on your phone's Appstore and install it.

Once you've installed it, open it up and login in to your amazon account. If you don't have any dealings with amazon before, then you'll have to create an account. After signing in to your account in the app, you'll have to search for you Echo Dot.

After selecting your Echo Dot, connect to Wi-Fi and follow the instruction it tells you. Then choose **continue**. The app will try to connect to the Echo Dot, once connected, include the Echo Dot in your Wi-Fi network and input the Wi-Fi network. Once you've finished setting up your Echo Dot, you'll have the privilege of using Alexa functions

You can get Alexa to do a lot of things, some things you can say to her from your Echo Dot are;

- 'Alexa, set a timer for 8 minutes' – Easy way to set a timer without actually touching the screen. Helpful when cooking
- 'Alexa, what the date?' – You just woke up and ;you have no idea if it's a week day or a week end
- 'Alexa, how is the traffic' – if you've already set up your address of home or work, in the settings, Alexa will be able to tell how the traffic situation is.
- 'Alexa, what's the weather forecast' – if you ask Alexa for weather forecasts

- without saying a particular place, it will give you the forecast for your location
- 'Alexa, Set an alarm for 5 a.m.' – no need to press or tap anything, just use Alexa to set an alarm with your Echo Dot
- 'Alexa, track my order' – Alexa will be able to track what you've ordered from amazon

Chapter 9
Using Alexa on Echo Show

If you want to set up the Echo, you'll have to install the Alexa app on your computer or smartphone. And just like the Echo Dot, this guy does not do stuffs offline. You'll need to make sure you have Wi-Fi connection and an account on amazon.

Make sure that you're not putting the show too far, try it to keep it not to near to the walls or window so that it can easily hear you. Connect it to power and follow the instructions it shows. Yes, good thing it has a screen, you'll be guided on what you should do to set up Wi-Fi, link to your amazon account, do the firmware updates and all the other necessary things you'll have to do.

If you've got an original Echo, you shouldn't have any problem with understanding the Echo Show. They work the same way with Alexa except for the part where the Echo show has screens and the Echo does not. It is said that the screen increases the functionality of the Echo Show.

Like for example, you get the gracious feature of being able to play movies and TV shows with Alexa. In fact you'll be able to browse the internet. You just get Alexa to open up a web browser and you start surfing. You also get a new advantage of being able to view certain skills.

Like the help it provides in the kitchen. **The Food Network** and other skills have upgraded their skill capabilities to be able to be used for efficiently I the kitchen

You can say these to Alexa with you eco show

- **'Alexa, play the trailer for The Legend of the Deceivers'** – Alexa then opens the trailer of whatever movie you ask to play
- **'Alexa, what movies are chowing nearby'** – Gives you the list of the moves that are being showed near you
- **'Alexa, what's the weather like today'** - Gives the weather forecast for the day

- **'Alexa, show me the lyric**'s – Supplies the lyrics f whatever song is played
- **'Alexa, call an Uber'** – Unlike the other screenless Echos, the Echo Show offer you the ability to be able to the updates about the status of your Uber ride.
- **'Alexa, take a photo'** – Yeah that's right you're able to take cool photos with your show. That means you don't have to set timer, your voice is enough to trigger the shutter.

Chapter 10

Using Alexa on your Amazon Tap

With your Amazon Tap it's really easy to use. You can put it anywhere you feel it comfortable to be in. In your bedroom, in the counter in the kitchen, in the living room couch, or just wherever you want it to be it.

If you want to use Alexa on your Tap,

1. You've got to first download and install the Alexa app on your mobile device (smart phone or tablet. If you get the Alexa app, you'll be able to manage the alarms you set, arrange your shopping list and control the music. For the requirements of the device,
   - Android has got to be 4.4 or it can be higher
   - Fire has to be OS 3.0 or it can be higher

- For iOS it has to be iOS 8.0 or it can be higher

If you want to get the Alexa app, you'll have to visit the App store for you own mobile device and install it

2. Now you'll have to put on your Tap. You'll have to connect the cable to the power adapter. Then you'll plug it to the Charging cradle which you'll connect to the power outlet.

3. In the Alexa app, connect your app to a Wi-Fi network. After setting up, you'll be able to talk to Alexa

You should recognize though that you cannot start taking to Alexa right away. You need to press something. You see the microphone button at the side of the device, you'll have to press that then you can begin to speak naturally to Alexa.

But that can get kind of hectic as you've got to be near the tap before you can actually give out commands to it. Amazon prepared for this in a way, you have the opportunity to turn on Hands-free mode. Nice, right? All you've got to say is

'Alexa' and the assistant will be more than ready to hear your commands.

To turn on the hands free mode
1. Enter the Alexa app
2. Go to **Settings** in the menu
3. Move to **Alexa devices** and chose your Tap
4. Hit the **Hands-free mode.**

With this feature you can start giving Alexa commands just like you would in the other Echos. You can follow this same process to turn it off.

Chapter 11

Using Alexa on Echo Connect

The Amazon Echo Connect is a cool new Echo device that enables you to use your Echo speaker as a speakerphone that you control with your voice. You can do the same thing with other Echos but this is different.

Other Echos only permit you to be able to make calls to other Echo users with their Echo devices. So it's an Echo to Echo thing. But with the Echo Connect, it's different, you'll be able to call contacts in your address book on your phone or a different landline. You can be able to place emergency call and even make international calls

If you want to call someone, it's just as easy and waking up Alexa and then saying the name of the contact to call. Before you use your Echo Connect you have to make sure of these

- That you've completed the setup for you VoIP service or you landline

- Put the Echo Connect somewhere near a power outlet and the Wi-Fi router
- If in your account you don't have a compatible Echo, you will see an error when setting up

1. Connect the power adapter to the Echo Connect and the plug it to the power outlet to turn the Echo Connect on
2. Plug the phone cable to the Echo Connect and then connect the other side to a Wi-Fi router or a phone jack or a telephone adapter.
3. Enter the Alexa app
- Then enter the **menu**
- Hit the **Devices** icon and tap the + button
- Choose **Add Device**
- Select **Amazon Echo** and choose your **Echo Connect** to connect your Wi-Fi

Now you can use your use your Echo Connect with your home's phone landline to call. One good thing about the Alexa app is that the contact stored in your phone will remain in sync. What this means is that Alexa can recall you contacts

Things to say to place phone call are

- **'Alexa, call Charles'** – this will place can to a particular person
- **'Alexa, dial 0 3 8 4 8 8 8 8 9'** – If you have the contact stored, you can just spell out the number
- **'Alexa, call 911'** – You can use Alexa to call the emergency service of your country
- You can also make a call to the pone type of a particular person like his work, or home. - **'Alexa, call Connor's cell phone'**

Chapter 12
Using Echo Spot with Alexa

After downloading the Alexa app and setting up your Echo spot, you will find that the default setting may not be up to your standard. You can still customize your Spot to give more functions.

To find ways personalize your Echo spot,
1. Enter the Alexa app
2. Slide to the **menu** and choose **Alexa Devices**
3. Select you're the Echo Spot

Form here, you'll be able to customize your Echo spot. Like you can modify the location of the device, the wake word for Alexa, the background, the language, the different sound and others.

One feature that many love to try out is the DND. This stands for **Do Not Disturb**. This does what it says, it doesn't disturb you. It will make you not to get notifications form the Echo Show or form Alexa, it will also turn off **Follow up mode**. This is the ability for Alexa to still hear you after saying a command. So you can call 'Alexa' give out your command and she'll still be waiting for you to give out more.

You can still use Alexa with the Echo Show to turn your home to a smart home and control your lights, fan, brew coffee. In fact you can even tell Alexa to turn on the TV for you. If you'd like to listen to instruction on recipes in the kitchen you can just get Alexa to play it for you

You could also set up your spot so that Alexa can recognize your voice. So that if you give out a command to call like 'Alexa, call Amber' Alexa will recognize your voice and go through your contacts and call Amber. This is the drop-in feature that allow you place video call to other Echos with screens

You can use Alexa to do a lot with your Echo spot. You can tell her to do stuff like you would on any other Echo. But you can also make use of some skills

- **'Alexa, play Dancers Village on Amazon Prime Video'** – If you've got a prime account, you can tell Alexa to play TV shows form there

- **'Alexa, call Sis on Skype'** – You have to enable the Skype skill
- **'Alexa, ask WikiHow how to sew my shirt'** – if you've enabled the WikiHow skill
- **'Alexa, ask Allrecipies for (say food) recipe'** – Enable the Allrecipe skill
- **'Alexa, what's my Flash briefing'** – If you've got a news service skill enabled
- **'Alexa, call an Uber'**

Chapter 13
Fun Things to do with Alexa

When you first got your Alexa device, you were probably shocked to see how humanely she responded to your request and the commands you gave out to her. Well you see, not only can you call her 'humanlike' you could say she's more like a superhuman. Though she's kind of new to game, she doesn't fail her users as she does almost all you tell her to do.

When you tell her to do your regular stuffs, she does so efficiently. But it's not only the formal things she can do, she can also do a bunch of cool stuffs too than many don't know about.

Routines

This will enable you to use your Echo to conform to your normal everyday routine. Okay what I'm trying to say is that you don't have to say, do this, do that before she can carry out your request.

Like when you just get home at night, you just say 'Alexa, I'm home' and she'll turn on the lights.

Depending on how you program her, Alexa can do a lot of things through Routines. Like the one we mentioned previously of turning on the light. You can could also tell her 'Good morning' and you'll wake up to your beloved songs, and get news at certain times. You can also get updates on traffic when you ask her.

Place video calls

With the screen enabled Echos, like the Echo Show and Echo spot that are also equipped with camera, you can also make video calls to devices you want. But for those who don't have the screen devices, this doesn't mean you can't make video calls

For those with an Echo dot or original Echo, you can still use the **Alexa app** to make video calls

Double to triple audio blast

There are many Alexa features that people don't know about. They just do the basic 'Alexa, play my music'. You can do much more to improve your music experience.

When you want to sit down and enjoy your favourite music and you have more than one Alexa device, you can connect and sync them together so that all of them will play the songs at the same time. That means an increased music quality in a way.

Let Alexa recognize you

Another cool thing about Alexa is that she can recognize different voices. When you talk she can idefity that it's you speaking. All you have to do to activate this option you just enter the Aex app and head over to the area titled 'Your Voice'

If there are several users of your Echo device, this can really come in handy. Apart for the reason you think this is beneficial, it can also act as safety. If somebody tries to purchase something with your account using your Echo, Alexa will not respond since it isn't your voice.

Get her to play music

If you would like to listen to music, you just have to say the word. If you want to listen any music, you just tell it to her, and it be offered to you.

You can say something like 'Alexa, play Pop' and she'll present it. If there's an artist you want to get their newest release, you can just tell Alexa something like 'Alexa, play the latest album by Rihanna' Alexa will give it to you obediently.

You'll be able to stream music form different music channels like amazon's own Amazon Music Unlimited. But you can enjoy other services too like Pandora or Spotify. You could even get radios like iHeartRadio or TuneIn Radio.

Equalizer

Back then when I just got a music player, I always fumbled around the settings looking for the equalizer. I see it and I don't know how to make adjustments. But with Alexa, you don't need to start tapping this, clicking that. You just give your command to Alexa.

You can tell her to reduce the treble, turn up the bass or to even set the mid range to 2. You can tell to do any modification you want to make. If you don't want to tell her but want to do it yourself,

1. Enter the **Settings**
2. Then select **Sounds**
3. Choose **Equalizer**

Get entertained with videos

With Alexa as your assistant, you can watch videos easily. She can easily find out the newest and hottest videos. Just tell her to update you about the new things on Prime video. You can also get her stream it to you own TV.

But you don't have to use **Amazon Prime** before you can enjoy videos, you can still get the benefit of third-party services.

Give your home gadgets the brains

Yeah Alexa can do bunch of cool stuffs but for many, nothing measures up to the ability to control their homes with her. Once you've connected your Echo to to your smart-home devices in the Alexa app, life will be a lot easier.

Now more getting up form bed when you're half asleep just to lock door. This can really piss one off. But now you're on a whole new level with Alexa, a simple 'Alexa, lock the front door' will do the trick. Or you can use her to control the lights

In the app, go to **Smart home**, then **Devices**. You'll be able to view your gadgets. You won't be able to use the advanced features but you will still be able to the basic things like controlling the air con

Controlling the color

With Alexa you can do more than just telling g her to turn on and turn off the lights. You can also adjust the hue of the lights. If you have a smart light that can change its color, you can say something like 'Alexa, make the lamp white' or you can change to different color and say 'Alexa, make the bedroom yellow'

If you go to the Alexa app, you'll be able to tweak the light too. Enter the **Alexa app** and select the option to **Set color button.** You'll find it just underneath the **main light control**

Chapter 14
Alexa Troubleshooting

NOTES:

Alexa doesn't connect to devices

Among the many capabilities of Alexa, one major ability is for her to connect to a wide range of smart devices. When connected, you may then use your voice to control how they work. These devices could be SmartThings, Wink, Philips, Honeywell and a lot of other manufactures

While using the device and controlling with your voice is really enjoyable, one thing that many have trouble with is actually connecting to use them.

1. One thing you want to ensure is that your Echo has to be compatible with your smart device. You may have to get the help of a bridge like the Wink hub
2. You can use **IFTTT. If This Then That** can help to with the connection
3. You also want to go through with the instruction to setup the smart device. It may even require that you get an app for the device to setup
4. Ensure that the devices are actually connected to your Wi-Fi network.

Alexa doesn't respond to calling

If you try to say the wake word for your Alexa device but she doesn't answer you, there are a few things you want to make sure of.

1. Be sure that the Echo device has power and it is connected to the internet.
2. The device should show a blue light and not red. If it shows a red light then the microphone is switched off. Hit the microphone button at the top

If you use multiple Echos and a different one answers you

1. You want to move the other Echo far from you and the one you want to respond, should be nearer to you
2. Just change the wake word for one of the device.

Alexa doesn't stream

One of the main reason why Alexa does not play music when you tell her to is because of a break in the internet connection. Another can be because of low ban with

1. If there are and evinces that are connected to the Wi-Fi and you are not using them, turn them off
2. Take away the device form the walls of your home and put it nearer o the wireless router
3. Put off the router and modem for about 30 seconds. Then you can turn both of them back on
4. Put off your Echo and after a while, put it back on

Alexa cut offs form Wi-Fi connection

This is another problem that some Echo users face. The Echo just suddenly disconnects itself from the Wi-Fi network. And you know if the Echo isn't connected to the internet it won't work

1. One thing you can do is to turn of the router and the modem for a few seconds. Then turn both on again
2. Turn off your Echo device to and turn it back on again
3. Try taking the Echo away from other devices. There a chance that there an interference in the connection. You can also decrease the interference by changing the speaker to the channel of 5GHz.

Alexa isn't hearing you well

When some get their Echos, they get a wonderful experience with Alexa. But overtime, it dawns on them that Alexa doesn't hear their commands well again.

1. For starters, you want to make sure that you're not crowding the Echo. Allow about 8 inches of space surrounding it
2. For some who got their Echos during winter, the Echo will probably not work as it previously would as the air conditioner will increase the noise in the room. So take Alexa away from any gadget that makes noise
3. You can do some voice training in the Alexa app. Go to **settings** in the app

Alarm sounds that Alexa gives are too loud

There's a chance that the alarms or notifications sounds that Alexa produces seem very loud or too quiet. You may have tried to reduce the playback volume in the Alexa app but it still continues to be loud.

Reason's because the playback volume doesn't not affect the timer, alarm or notification volume. So reducing or increasing it won't do anything to the alarm. So the question you will ask is, what then controls the alarm volume. To find that;
- Enter the **Alexa app**
- Enter the **Settings**
- Sect the name of your Echo
- Choose **Sounds**
- Now you'll see the different volumes. Reduce the one you want to be lowered.

Alexa doesn't connect Bluetooth

1. First make sure that your Echo device is not too far from the Bluetooth device you want to connect to. The distance between them should be at the 3 feet at the very least.
2. Very that your Bluetooth device is not at fault and is ready to pair
3. Restart your Bluetooth device and your Echo
4. Try to restart the connection again and see if there's an improvement

Trouble with Spotify

Alexa can play music form third-party music services and Spotify is one of them. Bu it seems Spotify tends to have more hitches then other services

There's no perfect antidote to this problem. But something worth doing is disconnecting your account on Spotify and log back in
- Enter **Settings** in the app
- Then **Music & media**
- Select **Spotify**
- Choose **Unlink account form Alexa** and confirm
- Select the option to **Link account on Spotify.com**

Alexa activates by itself

You might be watching a TV show and Alexa will suddenly respond to what is being said in the scene.

1. Try to place the Echo in place that's far from the TV
2. Use a different wake word for Alexa. You'll have the option to change to Amazon, Echo or Computer
3. Move your Echo away from the wall.

Disclaimer

In as much as the author believes beginners will find this book helpful in learning how to explore Alexa it is only a small book. It should not be relied upon solely for all Alexa tricks and troubleshooting.

About the author

Stephen Rock has been a certified apps developer and tech researcher for more than 12 years. Some of his 'how to' guides have appeared in a handful of international journals and tech blogs. He loves rabbits.

Facebook page @ Newcomers Guide

Also by the Author

1. IPHONE USER MANUAL FOR NEWCOMERS: All in one iOS 12 guide for beginners and seniors (iPhone, 8, X, XS & XS Max user guide)\
2. APPLE WATCH USER GUIDE FOR NEWCOMERS: The unofficial Apple Watch series 4 user manual for beginners and seniors
3. 3D PRINTING GUIDE FOR NEWCOMERS
4. SAMSUNG GALAXY S9 PLUS USER MANUAL FOR NEWCOMERS
5. WINDOWS 10 USER MANUAL
6. KINDLE FIRE HD MANUAL FOR NEWCOMERS
7. KINDLE FIRE 10 USER GUIDE FOR NEWCOMERS II

NOTES:

NOTES:

NOTES: